Summer Solutions.
Minutes a Day-Mastery for a Lifetime!

Level 8

English Grammar & Writing Mechanics

Nancy McGraw & Nancy Tondy

Bright Ideas Press, LLC
Cleveland, Ohio

Summer Solutions Level 8
English Grammar & Writing Mechanics

All rights reserved. No part of this publication may be reproduced or transmitted in any form or by any means, electronic or mechanical, including photocopy, recording, or any information storage or retrieval system. Reproduction of these materials for an entire class, school, or district is prohibited.

Printed in the United States of America

ISBN 13: 978-1-934210-09-3
ISBN 10: 1-934210-09-9

Cover Design: Dan Mazzola
Editor: Kimberly A. Dambrogio

Copyright © 2008 by Bright Ideas Press, LLC
Cleveland, Ohio

Instructions for Parents/Guardians

- *Summer Solutions* is an extension of the *Simple Solutions* Approach being used by thousands of children in schools across the United States.

- The 30 lessons included in each workbook are meant to review and reinforce the skills learned in the grade level just completed.

- The program is designed to be used 3 days per week for 10 weeks to ensure retention.

- Completing the book all at one time defeats the purpose of sustained practice over the summer break.

- Each book contains answers for each lesson.

- Each book also contains the *Help Pages* which list vocabulary, parts of speech, editing marks, rules for capitalization, punctuation, and spelling.

- Lessons should be checked immediately for optimal feedback.

- Adjust the use of the book to fit vacations. More lessons may have to be completed during the weeks before or following a family vacation.

Summer Solutions Level 8
English Grammar & Writing Mechanics

Reviewed Skills include:

- The Writing Process
- Proper Placement of Modifiers
- Gerund, Infinitive, and Participial Phrases
- Main and Subordinate Clauses
- Parallel Structure
- All Parts of Speech
- Verb Types, Subject-Verb Agreement
- Conjugation of Regular and Irregular Verbs
- Capitalization, Punctuation, and Spelling Rules
- Greek, Latin, and Anglo-Saxon Roots
- Connotation and Denotation
- Context Clues
- Cause and Effect / Fact and Opinion
- Similes, Metaphors, and Idioms
- Analogies, Synonyms, and Antonyms
- Avoiding Plagiarism

Help Pages begin on page 63.
Answers to Lessons begin on page 77.

Summer Solutions© Grammar & Writing **Level 8**

Lesson #1

Review the eight parts of speech. Write the name of each part of speech next to its definition. (Use the *Help Pages* if you need assistance.)

preposition   interjection   adverb   conjunction
noun   adjective   pronoun   verb

1. _____ expresses action or a state of being

2. _____ names a person, place, thing, or idea

3. _____ relates nouns or pronouns to other words in a sentence

4. _____ takes the place of a noun

5. _____ modifies (describes) verbs and other words; tells *when, how, where,* or *to what extent*

6. _____ modifies (describes) nouns or pronouns

7. _____ connects words, phrases, or clauses within a sentence

8. _____ a word or phrase that expresses strong feeling

9. What does the underlined phrase modify?

   <u>Having failed to read the directions</u>, the end result was a disaster!

   A) result
   B) end result
   C) disaster
   D) Nothing – it is a dangling modifier.

10. **Comparative adjectives**, such as "more graceful" and "shorter" are used to compare how many items?

   _____

   Superlatives, such as "swiftest" and "most pleasant" are used to compare how many items?

   _____

11. Use context clues to decide the meaning of the underlined word.

   The accusations against Mr. Thurman were clearly <u>unsubstantiated</u>, so the judge decided to release him.

   A) not proven   B) believable   C) remarkable   D) amusing

12. Draw each editing mark next to its meaning. (Check the *Help Pages* if you don't remember the symbols.)

   _____ capitalize   _____ add end mark

   _____ add something   _____ indent or start paragraph

   _____ take out something   _____ make lower case

Summer Solutions© Grammar & Writing — Level 8

Lesson #2

The Four Sentence Types

Declarative	Interrogative	Imperative	Exclamatory
Statement	Question	Command / Request	Strong Emotion
ends in a period	ends in a question mark	usually ends in a period	ends in an exclamation point
Coaster World is open for the summer.	What is the admission price?	Check the newspaper for information about ticket prices.	You can ride the fastest roller coaster in the world!

Write *declarative, interrogative, imperative,* or *exclamatory* next to each sentence.

1. _____ Put all the equipment in the locker room for now.

2. _____ This stuff weighs a ton!

3. _____ Who has the key to the locker room?

4. _____ The door at the end of the hallway is open.

5. Draw a line between the complete subject and the predicate.

    Six out of every ten kids drink chocolate milk at lunchtime.

6. Linking verbs connect the subject with a predicate noun or predicate adjective.

    Mrs. Edwards (was) late.
        linking verb   predicate adjective

    Circle the linking verb; underline the predicate adjective.

    We were ready, so we started doing our warm-up exercises.

Summer Solutions© Grammar & Writing   Level 8

7. **A nominative case pronoun is used as a <u>subject</u> or <u>predicate nominative</u>.**
   Choose the nominative case pronouns that will correctly complete this sentence.

   I know Joyce very well; (her / she) and (I / me) have been skating partners for many years.

8. **An objective case pronoun is used as an <u>object</u>.**
   Underline the objective case pronoun that will correctly complete this sentence.

   Dad will be driving, so give the directions to (him / he) or Ben.

9. Circle two synonyms. Use a dictionary if you need help.

   unsympathetic   curious   auspicious   inquisitive

10. Underline the verb phrase; write *main* or *helping* to label each verb.
    Example: Victor <u>will show</u> the film.
                      helping   main

    Eileen and I should arrive on time.

11 – 12. A phrase is a group of words that does not have a subject and a predicate; a clause has both a subject and a predicate. Write *phrase* or *clause* next to each item below.

   A) _____ that he was riding   C) _____ after the crash

   B) _____ sliding down further   D) _____ while she waited

Lesson #3

1. **The complete subject includes the subject and all its modifiers.** Underline the complete subject.

    Bright red, white, and blue decorations hung from the trees and lampposts.

2. **A writer may use examples to illustrate the meaning of a word.** Use context clues to determine the meaning of the underlined word.

    The squalid basement was filled with soiled rags, grubby old toys, and dusty boxes.

    A) used   B) filthy   C) miscellaneous   D) wet

3. **A writer may use antonyms or contrasts as context clues.** Use context clues to help you choose the meaning of the underlined word.

    Try not to be so derogatory; instead, say something kind.

    A) complimentary   B) compassionate   C) comical   D) insulting

4. Put a check next to any sentences that contain linking verbs.

    _____ A) Lincoln Middle is a Blue Ribbon school.

    _____ B) The teams from Lincoln win academic competitions every year.

    _____ C) Many of its sports teams are excellent also.

5. Underline the action verbs. Circle the linking verbs.

    Doreen asked for help as soon as she saw that the task would be overwhelming. That was smart!

6. Underline the words that could be used as prepositions.

    attract   outside   easily   throughout   window   beyond   over

7. Circle the simple subject and underline the prepositional phrase that modifies it.

    The willow with its long flowing branches provides plenty of shade.

8 – 12. Use the graphic organizer below to write a draft about the causes and effects of insomnia (inability to sleep). Use cause and effect signal words in some of your sentences.

Cause and Effect Signal Words and Phrases

can give rise to	caused by	resulting from	since	therefore
can lead to	due to	stemming from	so	then
can result in	stems from	as a result	thus	consequently
because of this	may cause	leads to	hence	because

Causes and Effects of Insomnia	
Causes	Effects
Consuming too much caffeine	Sluggishness during the day
Irregular sleep schedules	Falling asleep in class
Physical discomfort	Inability to concentrate
Anxiety, depression	Headache, irritability, eyestrain

_____
_____
_____
_____
_____
_____
_____
_____
_____
_____

Summer Solutions© Grammar & Writing **Level 8**

Lesson #4

1. Circle the subject and underline the prepositional phrase that modifies it.

    The houses along the lake have big back yards.

2. Is it a linking verb or an action verb?

    linking → The directions *look* complicated.

    action → If you need towels, *look* in the linen closet.

    Which contains a linking verb?

    A) Harry smelled smoke. C) Both
    B) The room smelled musty. D) Neither

3. Underline all the adjectives. Add commas where they are needed.

    Perry bought red green and yellow peppers; they're beautiful.

4. **Identifying Sentence Parts:** Look at the underlined words in the sentence. Then match the letter of the underlined words with the sentence parts listed below.

    Radia Perlman, born in 1952, was instrumental in the development of the internet.
    　　A.　　　　　　　　　　　B.　　C.　　　　　　　　D.

    _____ object of a preposition

    _____ predicate adjective

    _____ subject

    _____ linking verb

5. A clause is group of words that has both a

    _____ and a _____.

6. Underline the complete predicate.

    The seventy-year-old house sits atop a forested hill.

For the next three sentences, correct any errors in grammar, punctuation, capitalization, or spelling. Put a star next to the sentence if it has no error.

Examples: ~~Him~~ He and my dad are cousins.

Rachel ^has been the team captain lots of times.

7. Davietta brought beach towels for herself and I.

8. Please put all of there camping gear in the car.

9. Look toward the horizon; we seen dolphins out there!

10 – 12. Review the prefixes by placing them correctly in the chart. Then write an example of a word with each prefix. The first one has been done for you.

hemi   photo   biblio   ped

Prefix	Meaning	Example
biblio	book	bibliography
10.	light	
11.	foot	
12.	half	

Summer Solutions© Grammar & Writing **Level 8**

Lesson #5

1. **A writer may use synonyms to show the meaning of a word in context.** Use context clues to help you choose the meaning of the underlined word.

    An artistic person can put together an <u>aesthetic</u> design.

    A) demanding   B) creative   C) decrepit   D) tricky

Read the section entitled, "Avoiding Plagiarism," in the *Help Pages* to find the answers to the following questions.

2. The illegal use of someone else's words is called _____.

3. A list of sources that you used to get information for a report or research paper is called a _____.

4. A book is considered a "source." List three more examples of sources.
    _____

5. Underline the prepositional phrase.

    The map at the new Welcome Center will show where we are.

6. Look at the prepositional phrase you underlined above.

    A) What is the **preposition**? _____

    B) What is the **object** of the preposition? _____

    C) What word does the prepositional phrase modify? _____

7. Underline the pronouns in the following sentence.

    He and Marsha sent you an invitation to their party, didn't they?

8. Rewrite each phrase with the possessive form of the noun.

the quarters of the captain → _____

the playground of the children → _____

9. Always use a comma before a coordinate conjunction. Add the commas.

The Bentleys bought a house on our street and they moved in over the summer. The family is large but the kids are all a lot younger than I am. I introduced myself right away so Mrs. Bentley would know that I am available to baby-sit.

Complete the table below. All the information you need is in the *Help Pages*.

Pronoun Case			
Case	Use	Singular forms	Plural forms
Nominative	subject or predicate nominative	I, you, he, she, it, who	10.
Objective	direct object or object of a preposition	11.	us, you, them, whom
Possessive	12.	my, mine, your, yours, his, her, hers, whose, your, yours	our, ours, their, theirs, its, whose

Lesson #6

Complete the graphic organizer by placing the nouns in their proper categories.

Hawaiians   websites   officer's   George
Virginians' women's   Melissa's   telephone

		Singular	Plural
1.	Common		
2.	Proper		
3.	Common Possessive		
4.	Proper Possessive		

5. List the three <u>perfect forms</u> of the verb *see*. Use the subject *They*.

   _____   _____   _____

6. ***Connotation* is a word's emotional, implied, or suggested meaning.** What is the connotation of the word *volatile* in the next sentence?

   The dog's reaction is always *volatile* when strangers come to the door.

   A) hot-tempered   B) on fire   C) chemical

7. **A transitive verb sends its action to a direct object.** Circle the transitive verb, underline the indirect object, and put a box around the direct object.

   When Cherise handed me the envelope, it seemed heavy.

8. Correct the subject-verb agreement in the following sentence.

   Grady, along with everyone else on the team, are coming over after the game.

9. Underline the adjective clause; circle the noun it modifies.

The girls who ran the carwash made enough money to pay for the bus trip.

10 – 12. **Identifying Parts of Speech:** Decide which part of speech each underlined word represents. Then write the word on the line next to its part of speech.

Either Nicholas or Tremaine always brings freshly baked cookies for their entire baseball team.

A) noun → _____   D) transitive verb → _____

B) adverb → _____   E) pronoun → _____

C) adjective → _____   F) conjunction → _____

Lesson #7

1. Look for examples in the context clues; then choose the word that means about the same as the underlined word.

    Smoking cigarettes causes emphysema, cancer, heart disease, and other <u>maladies</u>.

    A) fumes
    B) heart attacks
    C) illnesses
    D) habits

2. Fill in the present progressive of the verb *practice*.

    Tino _____ _____ his fast pitch.

3. Is the following statement a fact, an opinion, or both?

    Andy Warhol's Pop Art transformed ordinary objects into something extraordinary.

    fact   opinion   both

4. Which sentence uses parallel structure?

    A) The design was fresh, exciting, and eye-catching.
    B) We used it for advertising, put it on letterheads, and signs.
    C) Both use parallel structure.
    D) Neither uses parallel structure.

5. What does the adverb phrase modify? _____

    We planted flowers *between the fence posts*.

6. Write **A** if the verb is active; write **P** if it is passive.

    _____ The Tigers won!   _____ All of the runs were scored in the final inning.

7. A *main clause* is also called a(n) _____ clause.

8. Draw a line through the prepositional phrases. Circle the simple subject.

   All of the apples near the top of the tree are ripe.

9. Use the editing mark for capitalization to show which words should be capitalized.

   mr. frost replied, "yes, i'll take two tickets please."

10 – 12. Study the chart and fill in the missing forms.

Principal Parts of Regular Verbs

Present	Past	Present Participle	Past Participle
sign	A)	signing	has/have/had signed
abbreviate	abbreviated	B)	has/have/had abbreviated
C)	D)	selecting	has/have/had selected
shovel	E)	F)	has/have/had shoveled

Summer Solutions© Grammar & Writing **Level 8**

Lesson #8

Add commas wherever they are needed.

1. Felix the restaurant owner has offered to sponsor our team.

2. We want to ride the roller coasters not the merry-go-rounds!

3. Look the funhouse is open. Let's get in line so we can be first.

4. Underline the passive verb; circle the doer of the action. Follow the example below.

    We <u>were soaked</u> by a sudden (cloudburst.)

    The car was chased by the local police.

5. Underline the adverb phrase and circle the verb it modifies. Follow the example below.

    Kenny (hit) the ball <u>over the fence</u>.

    The baseball flew out of the park.

6. Look at the adverb phrase you underlined in the item above. What does it tell?

    when   where   how   to what extent

7. Review the roots by placing them correctly in the chart.

chromo   dict   contra   fract

Roots	Meaning
A)	speak
B)	color
C)	break
D)	against

8 – 12. What is your favorite summer memory? Write about it here.

I remember… _____

_____

_____

_____

_____

_____

_____

_____

_____

_____

Summer Solutions© Grammar & Writing Level 8

Lesson #9

1. Underline the pronoun; circle its antecedent.

    The little (bird) couldn't fly because <u>its</u> wing was broken.

2. **An adjective phrase modifies a noun or a pronoun.** Underline the adjective phrase.

    Write your name <u>on the sign-in sheet</u> at the office counter.

    What noun does the adjective phrase modify? _____

Verbal:	How it is Formed:	Part of Speech:	Function within a Sentence:	Examples:
participle	present or past participle (verb)	adjective	modifies a noun (or pronoun)	The **fading** colors looked drab against the freshly **painted** walls.
gerund	present participle (ends in –ing)	noun	subject direct object object of a preposition predicate noun	**Cycling** is a rigorous sport. Tanya practices **diving** twice a week. Spring is the best time for **training**. My sport is **running**.
infinitive	base verb + "to"	noun	subject direct object object of a preposition predicate noun	**To sing** in a band is Lyn's ambition. Terrance just wants **to play**. Use it for anything except **to cut**. My preference is **to study**.
		adjective	modifies a noun modifies a pronoun	Choose a game **to play** at recess. Get someone **to help**.
		adverb	modifies a verb modifies an adjective modifies an adverb	**To open**, press here. Don't be afraid **to speak**. She is too clumsy even **to dance**.

Remember, a **gerund** is an *-ing* verb acting as a **noun**. A **participle** is an *-ing* verb acting as an **adjective**. A **progressive tense verb** also ends in *-ing*.

Write *gerund, participle,* or *verb* to show the function of the underlined word in each sentence.

3. <u>Barking</u> dogs are quite annoying.   _____

4. I told Nelson he was <u>barking</u> up the wrong tree.   _____

5. That constant <u>barking</u> is ruining my concentration.   _____

Summer Solutions© Grammar & Writing　　　　　　　　　　　　　　　　　　　　　　**Level 8**

6. Write **S** if the words are a sentence; write **F** if the words are a fragment.

   ___ Guess what!　　　___ School is cancelled.　　　___ And all activities!

7. Complete the analogy.　　air : atmosphere :: _____ : hydrosphere

   　　A) wind　　　B) fire　　　C) earth　　　D) water

8. Choose the correct verbs.

   Nuclear physics (is / are / were) one of the more challenging courses;

   therefore, a strong background in mathematics (is / are / were) essential.

9. Look at each underlined verb, and decide what type of verb it is. Then write *linking, action,* or *auxiliary* next to each letter below.

   Amy's dog, Milo, will sit, beg, perform tricks, and speak on command.
   　　　　　　　　A.　　　B.　　　　　　　　　　　　C.

   Amy believes that the dog is very intelligent, and she may even enter him
   　　　　　　　　　　　　　D.　　　　　　　　　　　　　　E.

   in a competition.

   A. _____　　　　D. _____

   B. _____　　　　E. _____

   C. _____

Identify each sentence type. (See the *Help Pages* for an explanation.)

　　A) simple　　B) compound　　C) complex　　D) compound-complex

10. ___ The weather is great, and although the water is cold, the beach is safe for swimming.

11. ___ We brought our swimsuits and some towels.

12. ___ You should use sunscreen even if the sky is cloudy.

19

Lesson #10

1. Underline the pronoun; circle its antecedent.

   As soon as they were finished, the musicians began to soak up the applause.

2. Which of the sentences uses parallel structure?

   A) After graduation, will you go to college, get a job, or become a volunteer?

   B) After graduation will you go to college, get a job, or are you considering volunteerism?

   C) Both use parallel structure.

   D) Neither uses parallel structure.

3. The **comparative degree** is used to compare _____ items.
   (How many?)

Write **T** if the sentence uses a transitive verb or **I** if the verb is intransitive.

4. _____ Gracie runs up and down the beach every morning.

5. _____ Kevin runs the shipping department at K.L.R. Press.

6. Underline the modifiers (adjective and adverbs) in this selection.

   Pattie walked gingerly through the magnificent gardens. She carefully inspected the exotic plants and studied the condition of the soil.

7. Look at the words you underlined in the item above. Write them in the correct category spaces here.

   adjective(s) → _____

   adverb(s) → _____

Complete the conjugation of the verb *rotate* in all 14 tenses, using *It* as the subject. Check the *Help Pages* if you want to see an example of a complete verb conjugation.

		Past	Present	Future
8.	Basic			
9.	Perfect			
10.	Progressive			
11.	Perfect Progressive			
12.	Emphatic			———

Summer Solutions© Grammar & Writing   **Level 8**

Lesson #11

Choose the possessive pronoun or verb that agrees with the indefinite pronoun in each sentence.

1. The teacher asked, "Does everyone have (their / her / they're) assignment?"

2. Either Jimmy or Marilyn (has / have) your project list.

3. See if somebody wants to give (they / his / their) presentation today.

4. For each clause, write **A** if the verb is active; write **P** if it is passive.

    _____ The muffins were made with the freshest ingredients, _____ and people bought them by the dozens.

5. Read the following sayings.

    A penny saved is a penny earned.

    Knowledge is power.

    Time is money.

    These sayings are all examples of which of the following?

         simile   metaphor   personification   hyperbole

6. Participles are verb forms that are used as _____.

    Participles modify _____ or _____.

Write *gerund, participle,* or *verb* to show the function of the underlined word in each sentence.

7. Do you know where my <u>editing</u> pen is? _____

8. <u>Editing</u> is an important part of the writing process. _____

9. We will be <u>editing</u> our essays this afternoon. _____

10. The **superlative degree** is used to compare _____ items.
    (How many?)

11. Use two editing marks to point out errors in the following sentence.

    The african violets will bloom continually as long as as you water and feed them.

12. Review these word parts by placing them correctly in the chart.

    onym   hydro   syn

	Greek Word Part	Meaning
A)		same
B)		water
C)		name

Summer Solutions© Grammar & Writing　　　　　　　　　　　　　　**Level 8**

Lesson #12

1. Underline the complete subject of the sentence below.

   Spending a few days at Disney World was the vacation of a lifetime!

   The complete subject is which of the following?

   A) gerund phrase   B) infinitive   C) plural noun   D) participial phrase

2. Draw a line through the prepositional phrases in the sentence below. Then circle the simple subject.

   A few of the girls on my softball team are high school freshmen.

3. Add the <u>future perfect form</u> of the verb *televise*.

   All of the re-runs in the series _____ _____ _____

   _____ by the time the new season begins.

4. Underline the adjective phrase and circle the word it modifies.

   The view from the front of the house is spectacular!

5. Correct this run-on by adding a semi-colon.

   Aqua Palace is a water park located just outside the city the park features super slides, a wave pool, and a sandy beach.

6. The sayings below are all examples of which of the following?

   Love is blind.　　Opportunity knocks.　　Diamonds are a girl's best friend.

   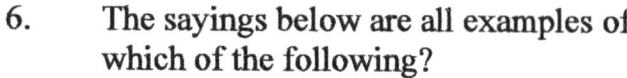
   onomatopoeia　alliteration　personification　hyperbole

7. Indicate whether the underlined words are used as verbs (**V**) or participles (**P**).

   A) _____ Each day the truck arrives at the <u>loading</u> dock.

   B) _____ Factory workers have been <u>loading</u> boxes in the warehouse.

   C) _____ The <u>loaded</u> containers are shipped to their destinations.

8. A word's denotation is what?

   A) its emotional meaning   B) its specific literal meaning

9. An adverb phrase modifies a _____, an _____,

   or an _____.

10 – 12. **Identify the sentence parts.**

<u>Woodridge High</u>, <u>my new school</u>, <u>was</u> the <u>location</u> of last year's statewide
    A.   B.   C.   D.

debate competition; some of the teachers <u>housed</u> <u>guests</u> who served as judges.
                                      E.   F.

_____ appositive   _____ linking verb

_____ simple subject   _____ direct object

_____ predicate nominative   _____ transitive verb

Lesson #13

1. Rewrite the sentence with correct capitalization and punctuation.

    would you like to try the alaskan whitefish asked the waiter

    _____

    _____

2. Add a colon and commas.

    Aunt Josie brought everything party favors hats games and food!

3. Circle the conjunction in the sentence below.

    It's pretty hot outside although there is a lovely breeze.

    What type of conjunction did you circle?

        coordinate   subordinating   correlative

4. Underline the gerund in the following sentence.

    Shopping is Margaret's favorite pastime.

5. What is the function of the gerund in the sentence above?

       subject   direct object   predicate noun   object of a preposition

6. This sentence has a misplaced modifier; rewrite the sentence so that the meaning is clear.

    Daily exercise keeps the animals mentally and physically engaged in the Nature Exhibit.

    _____

7. Underline the complete subject; write an S above the simple subject.

    Several of the varieties of food served on the cruise were unfamiliar.

Underline each infinitive. Indicate whether the infinitive is used as a noun, an adjective, or an adverb.

8. To operate, press the "start" button.   noun   adjective   adverb

9. Nathan needs a life jacket to wear during the drill.   noun   adjective   adverb

10. Olivia, try to remember what I told you.   noun   adjective   adverb

11. Review these roots and their meanings by placing them correctly in the chart.

    right   secret   deity

	Root	Meaning
A.	crypt	
B.	recti	
C.	theo	

12. Underline the reflexive pronoun, and circle its antecedent. (See the *Help Pages* to review pronouns.)

    Dad spilled red paint all over himself; he looked like a big tomato!

Lesson #14

1. Complete the analogy.   tree : figs :: _____ : grapes

   A) vine   B) juice   C) bush   D) fruit

2. Underline the gerunds in the following sentence.

   Bobbie likes gardening, but Jeff prefers painting.

   How are the gerunds used in the sentence?

   subjects   direct objects   predicate nouns   objects of a preposition

3. Match these word parts with their meanings.

   A) hemi   B) biblio   C) chrono

   half _____   time _____   book _____

4. What is the structure of the sentence below?

   The mayor is near the end of his term, but he will move forward with the project if he is re-elected.

   simple   compound   complex   compound-complex

In each sentence, underline the adverb clause and circle the word it modifies.

5. Please watch your sister until I get home.

6. As soon as you finish eating, wash all of the dishes.

7. Underline the infinitive. What word does the infinitive modify?

   It's really hot out here, so make sure you have something to drink.

   _____

8 – 12. **Tic-tack-toe Brainstorming:** Pick any three boxes – vertically, diagonally, or horizontally – and weave those words into a short paragraph. Use the example below or create your own tic-tac-toe chart. Don't think too much; just start writing.

skate board	cotton candy	horseback riding
geometry	puppies	friendship ring
porcupine	tree house	limousine

Lesson #15

1. Underline the gerund phrase.

   Hank is working very hard at <u>pleasing the new boss</u>.

   How is it used?

   subject   predicate noun   direct object   **object of a preposition**

2. Rewrite this sentence with proper placement of modifiers.

   The 100% cotton boys' shirts are on sale today.

   _____

   The boys' 100% cotton shirts are on sale today.

3. Which of the following is used in the sentence below?

   alliteration   **idiom**   simile   metaphor   personification

   Latoya will probably get the job; she certainly has all of her ducks in a row.

4. Choose the item which will give the sentence parallel structure.

   This summer I will work on my Eagle Scout badge by

   A) finishing my merit badges, service plan, and making a list of my leadership experiences.

   B) completing my merit badges and designing a service plan, and I will record my leadership experiences.

   C) completing my merit badges, developing a service plan, and documenting my leadership experiences.

   D) Any of the above will complete the sentence with parallel structure.

Summer Solutions© Grammar & Writing — Level 8

Identify the parts.

Travis is <u>waxing</u> his <u>car</u>. Next, he'll shine it with a <u>polishing</u> cloth.
           A.   B.   C.

He wants <u>to get</u> the car all set <u>for</u> his big <u>date</u>.
        D.   E.   F.

5. ____ object of a preposition   ____ participle

6. ____ preposition   ____ direct object

7. ____ progressive verb   ____ infinitive

Complete the conjugation of the verb *watch* in all 14 tenses, using *She* as the subject. Check the *Help Pages* if you want to see an example of a complete verb conjugation.

		Past	Present	Future
8.	Basic			
9.	Perfect			
10.	Progressive			
11.	Perfect Progressive			
12.	Emphatic			———

Lesson #16

1. Review these roots by placing them correctly in the chart.

   morph   caca   anthropo

Greek or Latin Word Part	Meaning
A.	harsh / evil / wrong
B.	people
C.	form

2. Add commas.

   Send your story to Dr. Sally Green Ph.D. at the college in Cloverleaf Georgia.

3. Underline the adverb in the sentence below.

   Nicky approached the magnificent gate apprehensively.

   Which word does the adverb modify? _____

4. Underline the gerund.

   Driving is a privilege that comes with many responsibilities.

   How is the gerund used in the sentence?

   subject   predicate noun   direct object   object of a preposition

5. Draw a line through any prepositional phrases. Then circle the simple subject.

   Most of the pictures in our yearbook are in color.

6. List seven coordinate conjunctions.

   _____

7. Read this proverb from Zaire, Africa.

   No matter how full the river, it still wants to grow.   ~African Proverb

   What type of figurative language is used in the proverb?

   personification   simile   metaphor   hyperbole   alliteration

8. Use editing marks to identify three errors in the following sentence.

   Their are my shoes; molly and I been looking all over for them!

9. Write **P** if the words are a phrase; write **C** if the words are a clause.

   _____ if we win   _____ next to the goal line

10 – 12. Identify the sentence parts.

   After <u>planting</u> the seedlings, it is <u>important</u> <u>to water</u> often <u>until</u> the young
            1.   2.   3.   4.

   roots are well established. Fast <u>growing</u> trees <u>thrive</u> in moist soil.
                                     5.   6.

   A) _____ intransitive verb

   B) _____ participle

   C) _____ predicate adjective

   D) _____ subordinating conjunction

   E) _____ infinitive

   F) _____ gerund

Summer Solutions© Grammar & Writing Level 8

Lesson #17

1. A participle acts as which part of speech?

    A) noun   B) adjective   C) adverb   D) any of these

2. Which word means the opposite of the underlined word?

    Luke's dad is very <u>jovial</u>; he's always smiling and telling jokes.

    A) ebullient   B) pessimistic   C) lighthearted   D) buoyant

3. The pronoun does not agree with its antecedent in the following sentence; rewrite the sentence correctly.

    The committee elected their new chairman today.

    _____

4. Which sentence has parallel structure?

    A) We play guitar, flute, drums, and sing.

    B) We sing, play instruments, and have made a CD.

    C) We sing songs, and we play guitar, flute, and drums.

    D) All three have parallel structure.

5. Fix the run-on by inserting a semi-colon.

    Scientists employ a strategy called the *scientific method* which is a systematic approach to gathering information and solving problems there are six steps in the scientific method.

34

6. What does the underlined phrase modify?

   Experimenting, <u>one of the steps of the scientific method</u>, is a way to test one's hypothesis.

   A) Experimenting   B) hypothesis   C) It is a dangling modifier.

7. Underline the conjunction in the sentence below.

   Scientists must make careful observations during an experiment because they will need to analyze the data they've gathered.

   What type of conjunction is it?   coordinate   subordinating   correlative

8. Find the <u>implied metaphor</u> in the following sentence.

   We lost our game against the Penguins, and that extinguished any hope of making it to the play-offs.

   The verb *extinguished* tells you that "hope" is being compared to what?

   A) fire   B) optimism   C) winning   D) water

9. Choose the correct verb.

   Near the edge of town, in the lush green woods, (stand / stands) a three hundred year old oak tree.

   What is the simple subject of the sentence in the item above? _____

In each sentence, underline the infinitive phrase. Then indicate whether the infinitive phrase is used as a noun, an adjective, or an adverb.

10. To transfer calls, enter the phone number and pound sign.   _____

11. Jay attempted to remove the tire with a crowbar.   _____

12. Do we have some bread to serve with dinner?   _____

Lesson #18

1. A gerund acts as what part of speech?

    noun   adjective   adverb   any of these

2. This sentence has a dangling modifier; rewrite the sentence so that the meaning is clear.

    In the new kitchen, Felicia can watch the birds washing dishes.

    _____

    _____

3. Underline the transitive verb, circle the indirect object, and put a box around the direct object.

    Volunteers gave the runners water and snacks at stations along the route.

4. Fill in the future perfect tense of the verb *travel*.

    By the time we get to Florida, we _____ _____ _____ through six different states.

5. What is the function of the underlined word?

    If it starts to rain, we can move the party <u>inside</u>.

    adverb   preposition   adjective   verb   subordinating conjunction

6. Combine these sentences to make one compound-complex sentence.

    Every year we go to a theme park. We always have a great time. I really want to visit the Grand Canyon.

    _____

    _____

7. Underline the adverb clause.

> Natasha excels when she applies herself.

What word does the clause modify? _____

8. Underline the adjective clause; circle the word it modifies.

> The fence that separates our properties is rusty and full of holes.

Use the following sentence to complete the next two items.

> The hurricane may reach the coast by morning, but some of the tourists will need hotel rooms since there are not enough flights to get everyone out of the city today.

9. How many clauses are in the sentence? _____

What type of sentence is it?

> simple   compound   complex   compound-complex

10. Put a box around the verb(s) in each clause.

11. Choose the pronoun that renames the subject.

> The swimmers (who's / whose / whom) diving lessons are today will go to lunch first.

12. Use editing marks to correct three capitalization errors.

> During the Summer, a place called Death Valley in California has the hottest temperatures in the western hemisphere.

Lesson #19

1. Review these roots by placing their meanings correctly in the chart.

   fire   measure   writing

	Root	Meaning
A.	igni	
B.	meter	
C.	gram	

2. Choose the ending that makes the sentence clear.

   Mr. and Mrs. Chen are martial arts masters; no one is more qualified (than them / than they).

3. Which of the following sentences is punctuated correctly?

   A) "Where's the fire," shouted Thomas?

   B) Use three fourths cup of water, and a teaspoon of salt.

   C) Everything was gone: jewelry, cash, and electronics.

   D) All are punctuated correctly.

Write *fact*, *opinion*, or *both* next to each statement.

4. _____ While at least one science credit is required, the smartest kids in high school take several science classes.

5. _____ Chemistry is difficult; however, students always enjoy the lab work.

6. _____ On a survey, 30% of the juniors chose biology as their favorite subject.

7. Underline the infinitive. Is the infinitive used as a noun, an adjective, or an adverb?

   Life is a great teacher, and there are so many important lessons to learn.

   noun   adjective   adverb

8 – 12. Should physical education be a requirement in high school? ____ yes ____ no

   Write a short persuasive essay which supports your opinion.

Lesson #20

1. Choose the correct verb.

   One of the plants – either the ivy or the African violet – (need / needs) water.

2. Combine the following sentences to create <u>one</u> complex or compound-complex sentence.

   Fish have backbones. Jellyfish have the word "fish" in their name. Jellyfish do not have backbones.

   _____

   _____

3. Which sentence is punctuated correctly?

   A) On the first day of school, Keisha forgot her locker number; even though she had just practiced opening her locker, at orientation the day before!

   B) The school custodian was very kind, and he helped by directing Keisha to the guidance counselor.

   C) Once she got the combination – Keisha opened the locker easily – but she was still late for class!

   D) All of the sentences are punctuated correctly.

4. Underline the simple subject.

   Under the porch steps, a litter of kittens snuggled against its mother.

5. Complete the analogy.

   calf : dolphin :: fawn : _____

Cross out or circle an error in each of the next two sentences. Write a correction above each error.

6. Someone as experienced as yourself will have no trouble chairing the committee.

7. There is plenty of fruit juice, danish pastry, and yogurt on the breakfast table.

Complete the conjugation of the verb *study* in all 14 tenses, using *They* as the subject. Check the *Help Pages* if you want to see an example of a complete verb conjugation.

		Past	Present	Future
8.	Basic			
9.	Perfect			
10.	Progressive			
11.	Perfect Progressive			
12.	Emphatic			—

Summer Solutions© Grammar & Writing   Level 8

Lesson #21

1. Write the proper citation for this book. (See the Bibliography Guide in the *Help Pages*.)

    - *The Happy Prince and Other Fairy Tales*
    - Written by Oscar Wilde
    - Published by Courier Dover Publications, in New York in 2001

    _____

    _____

Read this quote by Oscar Wilde: "Keep love in your heart. A life without it is like a sunless garden when the flowers are dead."

2. What is the <u>connotation</u> of the word *heart* in the quote?

    internal organ   inner being   kindness   a type of pump

3. Which of the following is used in the quote?

    simile   metaphor   personification   alliteration   idiom

Write *gerund, participle,* or *verb* to signify the function of the underlined word in each sentence.

4. <u>Speaking</u> is impossible when you are having a tooth filled. _____

5. Germaine hopes to get a <u>speaking</u> part in the play. _____

6. Nan has been <u>speaking</u> for the past hour! _____

7. Underline the complete subject.

    To build a new house has been a goal of ours for a long time.

    The complete subject is which of the following?

    A) gerund phrase   B) infinitive phrase   C) noun phrase   D) participial phrase

8. Fill in the past emphatic form of the verb *find*.

You were right; Sandy _____ _____ a gold necklace on the beach!

9. Choose the correct adjective in each clause.

Noreen is the (elder / oldest) of the two sisters. Their brother, Niles, is the (younger / youngest) child in the family.

10. In which sentence are the modifiers most appropriately placed?

   A) A tattered blue baby's blanket was left in the car.

   B) A tattered baby's blue blanket was left in the car.

   C) A baby's tattered blue blanket was left in the car.

   D) A blue tattered baby's blanket was left in the car.

Write the next two sentences with correct capitalization and punctuation.

11. arlington national cemetery is a burial ground for american soldiers

   _____

   _____

12. the arlington estate in virginia once belonged to general robert e lee

   _____

   _____

Lesson #22

1. The pronoun agreement is incorrect in the following sentence. Cross out the part that is incorrect and write the correction.

    Please put everything back in their box, and rearrange the furniture.

2. Underline the participial phrase and circle the noun it modifies.

    Terrance is convinced that the girl running the ice cream stand has a crush on him.

Avoid double negatives; use only one negative in a clause.

Double Negative	Corrections
Karl didn't have no equipment.	Karl had no equipment. or Karl didn't have any equipment.
Doris couldn't hardly sing.	Doris could hardly sing. or Doris couldn't sing.
There wasn't but one road.	There was but one road. or There was one road.

Rewrite the sentences correctly.

3. One of the skills I never didn't master was ice-skating.

4. We're not allowed to wear no tennis shoes or sandals with our uniforms.

    _____

5. My dog was so sick; she wouldn't barely lift her head.

    _____

Summer Solutions© Grammar & Writing   Level 8

6. Choose the correct pronoun.

   I like to go out on the boat, but my brother likes water skiing more than (I / me).

Cross out or circle an error in each sentence. Then write the correction above it. If there is no error, put a star next to the sentence.

7. Tomorrow is a holiday; yourself and Cindy should get the day off.

8. For breakfast, we like to eat canadian bacon with eggs and cheese.

9. Indicate whether the voice of the verb in each clause is active or passive.

   _____ We were shown the entire exhibit, _____ and we viewed a short film.

10. Mark two spelling errors in the sentence; then write the words correctly.

    Felicia is taking a coarse at the recreation center, and she's working as a lifeguard at the comunity pool.

    _____

11 – 12. Examine the Greek or Latin roots in the words listed below; sort the words according to their meanings.

   temporal   chronological   cryptology   pyrotechnics   audiologist

   pedicure   moped   cryptic   ignition   flambeau

   Words that have to do with:

   Hearing → _____

   Feet → _____

   Secrets → _____

   Time → _____

   Fire → _____

45

Lesson #23

1. In the sentence below, what word does the underlined part modify?

   <u>After putting a fresh coat of paint on the garage</u>, the roof looks shabby.

       A) roof   C) looks

       B) shabby   D) It's a dangling modifier.

2. Is the sentence simple, compound, or complex?

   You may swim in the lake as long as the lifeguard is on duty.

       simple   compound   complex

3. Circle the conjunction. What type of conjunction is it?

   Bring the cooler down to the beach, so we can have a picnic.

       coordinate   subordinating   correlative

4. Complete the analogy.   magazine : periodical :: _____

       A) advertisement : sell   C) mail : post office

       B) news : reporter   D) documentary : film

5. List the information that is needed to write a book citation in a bibliography.

   _____

   _____

6. Based on context clues, choose the meaning of the underlined word.

   Spending a few hours on the beach without sunscreen can cause <u>superficial</u> burning. Long-term exposure to harmful UV rays however, can cause serious skin damage.

       A) on the surface   B) third degree   C) severe   D) life threatening

7. This sentence has a misplaced modifier. Rewrite the sentence clearly.

   Just then, a delivery man rang the doorbell with a double-cheese pizza.

   _____

   _____

8. Underline the transitive verb and circle the direct object.

   Rose woke the children early, so they would be ready on time.

9. What is the <u>function</u> of the underlined word?

   <u>Writing</u> scripts for television commercials is Lynn's specialty.

   adverb   noun   adjective   verb   subordinating conjunction

Cross out or circle an error in each sentence. Then write the correction above it.

10. The milk is to old; just look at the expiration date on the side of the bottle.

11. Mrs. McKinley has offered to drive Beverly, Patrice, and myself to our summer camp this year.

12. Circle the linking verb; underline the predicate nominative.

    My mother was the president of her own company after she retired from a career in nursing.

Summer Solutions© Grammar & Writing   **Level 8**

Lesson #24

1. Match these word parts with their meanings.

    A) mono   B) audio   C) pyro   D) neo

    new _____   one _____   fire _____   hearing _____

For the next two items, underline the infinitive phrase and indicate how the phrase is used.

2. Mrs. Milks finally decided to order new carpet for the children's playroom.

    subject   direct object   predicate nominative   object of a preposition

3. The goal of today's meeting is to schedule events for August.

    subject   direct object   predicate nominative   object of a preposition

4. What is the structure of the sentence below?

    Sharon is here today, and she will go over her report if time permits.

    simple   compound   complex   compound-complex

5. Complete the analogy.   relax : rest :: disagree : _____

    A) quarrel   B) grievance   C) argument   D) concur

6. Which spelling is correct? If neither is correct, write the word correctly.

    A) achieve   B) acheive   _____

7. Underline the gerund.

    Dancing is fun, so don't worry about how you look.

    What is its function in the sentence? _____

48

Summer Solutions© Grammar & Writing Level 8

8 – 12. Imagine that you are about to write a great novel. Create a biographical outline for one of your main characters by completing the graphic organizer below.

Character' Full Name _____

Nickname _____

Male _____   Female _____   Age _____

Occupation _____

Birthplace _____

Current Residence _____

Favorite Foods _____

Favorite Type Music _____

Favorite Movie _____

Life Goal _____

Most Embarrassing Moment _____
_____
_____

Fondest Memory _____
_____
_____

Summer Solutions© Grammar & Writing **Level 8**

Lesson #25

1. Find the <u>implied metaphor</u> in the following sentence.

    At every step a child should be allowed to meet the real experiences of life; the thorns should never be plucked from his roses. ~Ellen Kay

    In this quote, the speaker is comparing *roses* to what?

    A) pain   B) a garden   C) life experiences   D) hardships

2. Underline the complete subject; circle the simple subject. (Draw a line through prepositional phrases to isolate the simple subject.)

    One of the goals of the event was to raise money for the hunger center.

3. A gerund is a verb used as a(n) _____.

4. Underline the gerund phrases in the following sentence.

    The duties are typing letters, answering calls, and packing boxes.

    How are the gerund phrases used in the sentence?

    verbs   direct objects   predicate nominatives   objects of a preposition

5. Rewrite the sentence correctly.

    At <u>north</u> <u>park</u>, we (road)[sp] all the roller coasters at least ∧times.
    three

    _____

    _____

6. Which of the following sentences is punctuated correctly?

    A) When you go to the store, please buy: milk, bread, eggs, and cereal.
    B) I think we have everything else: cheese, muffins, fruit, and juice.
    C) Oh wait…it looks like we dont have coffee, or tea.
    D) Maybe, you should make a list?

7. This sentence has a misplaced modifier. Rewrite the sentence clearly.

A police officer chased a stray dog on horseback through the neighborhood.

_____

_____

_____

_____

Complete the conjugation of the verb *trust* in all 14 tenses, using *He* as the subject. Check the *Help Pages* if you want to see an example of a complete verb conjugation.

		Past	Present	Future
8.	Basic			
9.	Perfect			
10.	Progressive			
11.	Perfect Progressive			
12.	Emphatic			——

Summer Solutions© Grammar & Writing   **Level 8**

Lesson #26

1. Circle the linking verb; underline the predicate nominative.

    Since Norm became president, everything has been running smoothly.

2. Choose the sentence that has subject verb agreement.

    A) The marching band are practicing on the football field.

    B) The marching band is practicing on the football field.

    C) The marching band always practice on the football field.

    D) The marching band have practiced on the football field.

3. Draw a line to separate the complete subject and the predicate.

    A herd of buffalo grazing on the open plains was painted on the museum wall.

4. Write the plural of each noun.

    trophy   wolf   slice

    _____   _____   _____

5. Choose a nominative case pronoun.

    Carl saw Ms. Blaine, but he didn't realize that the person in charge was (she / her).

6. Which contains a linking verb?

    A) The vocals sound a little flat.

    B) The music director made us practice for an hour!

    C) Both contain linking verbs.

Proof It! Find two errors in each of the following sentences. Use editing marks to point out the errors.

7.   Kim always asks for german chocolate cake on her Birthday.

8.   Mom serves the cake with vanila bean ice cream and fresh coffee

9.   Add six commas.

   Poncho Sanchez a Latin jazz artist salsa singer and band leader was born on October 30 1951 in Laredo Texas.

Match each underlined word or phrase with its function below.

   Poncho Sanchez, <u>a gifted percussionist</u>, <u>was exposed</u> to popular <u>Latin</u>
                    A.   B.   C.

   music <u>while</u> he was growing up <u>in the Los Angeles area</u>. Sanchez learned
          D.   E.

   <u>to play the conga</u> as a young child.
        F.

10.   proper adjective → _____

   infinitive phrase → _____

11.   prepositional phrase → _____

   conjunction → _____

12.   appositive → _____

   passive verb → _____

Summer Solutions© Grammar & Writing Level 8

Lesson #27

Cross out or circle an error in each sentence. Then write the correction above it. If there is no error, put a star next to the sentence.

1. The captain was visibly distressed upon hearing the news that his ship had went south.

2. Uncle Alfred is my godfather because him and my dad have been friends since they were kids.

3. Jennie gets to make announcements since she speaks clear, and she is able to keep everyone's attention.

4. A *main clause* is also called an _____ clause.

5. What is the function of the underlined word?

    Next year, the producers will be <u>filming</u> various documentaries.

        gerund   particple   verb

6. Edit the sentence below with three different editing marks.

    Laura served french bread with the salads, and while she offered a delightful cheesecake for desert.

7. Use context clues to determine the meaning of the underlined word.

    All of the actors were horrified when they read the critic's <u>trenchant</u> remarks about their performance in the play.

    A) biting   B) complimentary   C) perceptive   D) humorous

Fill in the principle parts of the verbs.

	Present	Past	Present Participle	Past Participle
8.			bursting	
9.				forsaken
10.		sprang		

11 – 12. Write two cause-and-effect statements, based on the information in the graphic organizer. (See Lesson #3 for cause-effect signal words.)

Sources and Effects of Noise Pollution	
Sources of Noise	Effects of Noise Pollution
Work-related noise, construction	Distraction, inability to concentrate
Sports events, concerts	Anxiety, psychological discomfort
Airplanes, street traffic, lawn mowers	Stress, irritability, headache
Loud music, T.V., films in theaters	Hearing loss

Lesson #28

Identify the parts:

Genetics is the study of how traits are passed from one generation to the next.
A.   B.   C.   D.

By studying genes, researchers discover new ways to improve people's health.
E.   F.   G.   H.

1. _____ infinitive   _____ transitive verb

2. _____ subject   _____ direct object

3. _____ predicate nominative   _____ gerund phrase

4. _____ prepositional phrase   _____ passive verb

Label each of the next three sentences: *simple, compound, complex,* or *compound-complex.*

5. _____ Yesterday, the weather was perfect, and we had our ninth annual family reunion picnic at Firestone Park.

6. _____ This year there were over a hundred people at the reunion, including adults and children of all ages.

7. _____ The reunion picnic seems to get bigger each year even though many of my relatives have moved to other parts of the country.

8. Underline the transitive verb and circle the direct object.

    Each evening, the setting sun bathes the countryside in shades of crimson and ginger.

9. Complete the analogy.   stomach : digestive :: _____

    A) muscles : skeletal   C) feeling : nervous

    B) eyesight: vision   D) heart : circulatory

10. What is the subject of the sentence in the quote written below?

    Start by doing what's necessary, then what's possible, and suddenly you are doing the impossible.   ~ Francis of Assisi

    _____

11. Look again at the quote by Francis of Assisi. One of the underlined parts is a gerund phrase; the other is a verb and direct object. Which is which?

    Start by <u>doing what's necessary</u>, then what's possible,
                  A.

    and suddenly you are <u>doing the impossible</u>.
                  B.

    _____ gerund phrase   _____ verb + direct object

12. What is the function of the underlined word?

    The house sits on a one-acre lot <u>beside</u> a small lake in the suburb of Harwood.

        noun   preposition   adjective   verb   conjunction

Summer Solutions© Grammar & Writing Level 8

Lesson #29

Use the following quote to complete items 1 through 4.

> I pack my trunk, embrace my friends, embark on the sea, and at last, wake up in Naples, and there beside me is the stern fact, the sad self, unrelenting, identical, that I fled from. ~ Ralph Waldo Emerson

1. How many clauses are in the sentence? _____
   (Remember a clause has its own subject and predicate.)

   What type of sentence is it?

   simple   compound   complex   compound-complex

2. Which two verbs are transitive? _____

   What are their direct objects? _____

3. Which three verbs are intransitive? _____

4. What linking verb is used in the quote? _____

Write *fact*, *opinion*, or *both* next to each.

5. _____ According to a study by the National Dropout Prevention Network, 80% of prisoners in American jails are high school drop-outs.

6. _____ The study shows that people who drop out of high school are more likely to be arrested; that statistic alone should motivate kids to stay in school.

7. _____ High school dropouts really have no chance of succeeding in life.

Summer Solutions© Grammar & Writing **Level 8**

8 – 12. Take a look at the word web below. It lists some school-related concerns and issues. Use ideas from the web to write a paragraph about the start of a new school year.

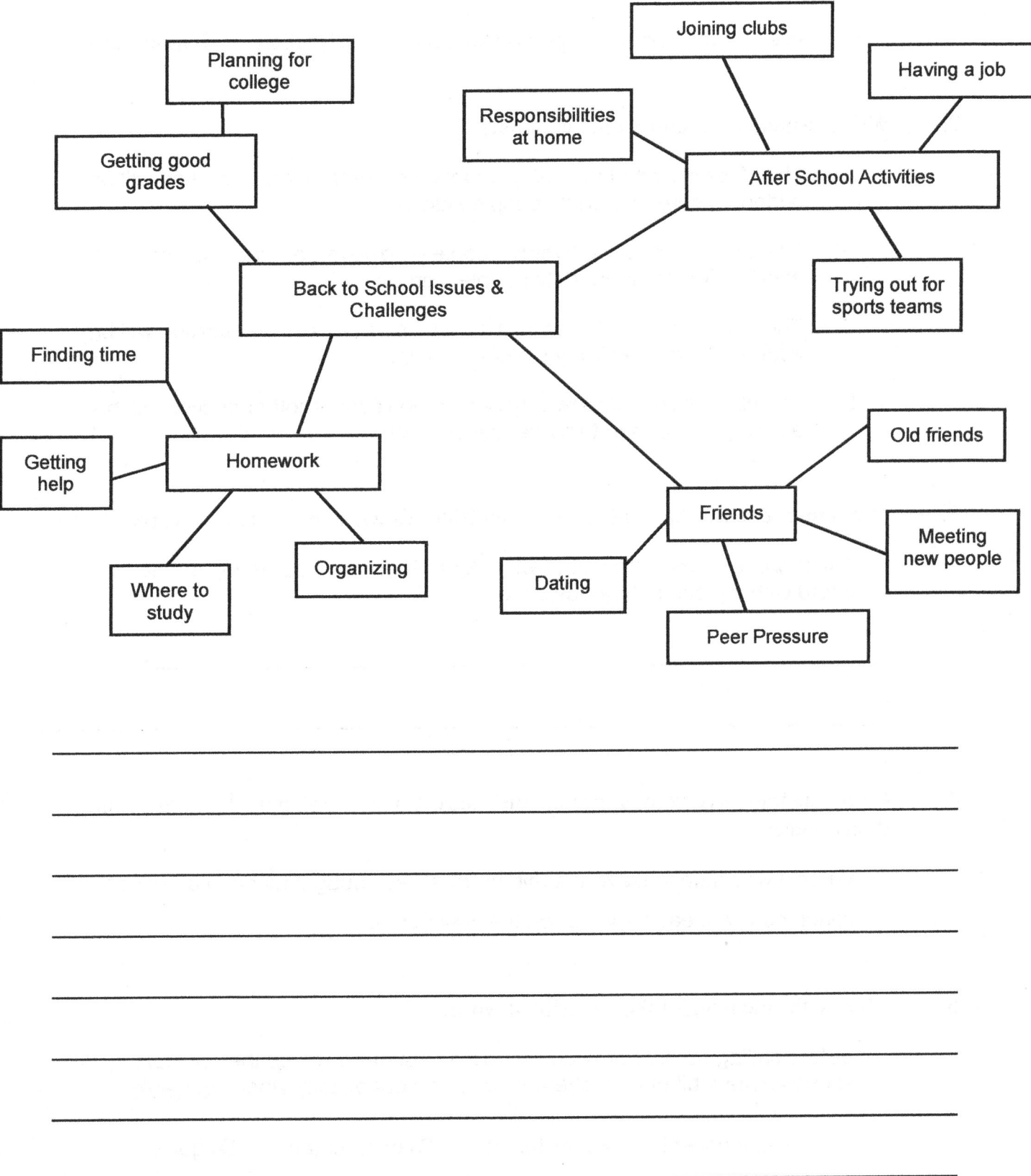

_____

_____

_____

_____

_____

_____

_____

Lesson #30

1. Identify the following:

   Autumn is a second spring where every leaf is a flower. ~Albert Camus

   simile   metaphor   personification   alliteration   hyperbole

2. Which sentence has correct punctuation?

   A) The class is limited to twenty people, however, another section will be added, if more than thirty people sign up.

   B) The class is limited to twenty people – however, another section will be added – if more than thirty people sign up.

   C) The class is limited to twenty people; however, another section will be added if more than thirty people sign up.

   D) The class is limited to twenty people however, another section will be added <u>if</u>, more than thirty people sign up.

3. The sentence below has a misplaced modifier. Rewrite the sentence clearly.

   A first grader came to the door while Mrs. Sherman was writing on the board with a piece of birthday cake.

   _____

   _____

4. Circle the transitive verb, underline the indirect object, and put a box around the direct object.

   When it was time to leave the fair, mom always bought us each a stick of cotton candy to eat in the car on the way home.

5. Choose the meaning of the underlined word.

   Before calling parents or accusing anyone of misconduct, the principal spends quite a bit of time attempting to find out exactly who is <u>culpable</u>.

   A) innocent   B) mistaken   C) persecuted   D) guilty

Summer Solutions© Grammar & Writing   Level 8

Match the Greek or Latin roots with their meanings.

     grand   acous   anti   magni   tempo
     syn   chrono   contra   audio   homo

6. Time → _____

7. Large → _____

8. Hearing → _____

9. Same → _____

10. Against → _____

11 – 12. Write *infinitive* or *gerund* next to each letter to identify the underlined parts. Then choose the word that names the function of the underlined words.

<u>Planning</u> air travel can be complicated, but here is one
  A.

thing you can do <u>to make</u> flying easier: Check ahead of
               B.

time with the airline <u>to learn</u> everything you can about
               C.

its travel guidelines. <u>Being prepared</u> will prevent hassles at the airport.
               D.

     A. _____   subject   direct object   adjective   adverb

     B. _____   subject   direct object   adjective   adverb

     C. _____   subject   direct object   adjective   adverb

     D. _____   subject   direct object   adjective   adverb

Level 8

English Grammar
& Writing Mechanics

Help Pages

Help Pages

The Eight Parts of Speech:
Adjectives modify nouns or pronouns. A proper adjective begins with a capital letter.
Adverbs modify verbs, adjectives, or other adverbs. Adverbs tell *how*, *when*, *where*, and *to what extent*.

Conjunctions connect similar words, clauses, or phrases within a sentence.
    Coordinate Conjunctions: and, or, nor, but, yet, for, so
    Subordinating Conjunctions join a subordinate clause with a main clause. See the chart at the bottom of this page.
    Correlative Conjunctions act in pairs.
        either/or, neither/nor, both/and, whether/or, not/but, not only/but also

Interjections are words or phrases that express strong feeling. **Examples:** Ouch! Gosh! Oh no!

Nouns name a person, place, thing, or idea. Nouns may be common or proper, singular or plural, abstract or concrete. A proper noun begins with a capital letter.
    Collective Nouns are words that name a "collection." A collective noun is singular and is treated as a single unit. <u>Collective nouns</u> used as subjects take *singular verbs*.
    Examples: the <u>family</u> *is*, the <u>orchestra</u> *plays*, a <u>committee</u> *studies*

Prepositions relate nouns or pronouns to other words in the sentence. For a list of common prepositions, see the chart below.
    A **Prepositional Phrase** begins with a *preposition* and ends with a <u>noun</u> or a pronoun.
    Examples: *against* the <u>fence</u>, *beside* <u>me</u>

Pronouns replace nouns. The pronoun *I* is always capitalized. Common pronoun types are described on p. 65.
Verbs convey action or a state of being. A verb is the main word in the predicate of a sentence. For an explanation of verb types, see p. 65.

Subordinating Conjunctions:					
after	as much as	even if	in order that	than, that	when
although	as soon as	even though	now that	though	whenever
as	as though	how	provided	till	where
as if	because	if	since	unless	wherever
as long as	before	inasmuch as	so that	until	while

Some Common Prepositions:					
about	around	down	instead of	over	toward
above	before	during	into	out	under
across	behind	except	near	outside	underneath
across from	below	for	nearby	past	until
after	beneath	from	next to	since	up
against	beside	in	of	through	upon
along	between	in back of	off	throughout	with
alongside	beyond	in front of	on	to	within
among	by	inside	onto	together with	without

Help Pages

Pronouns:
Demonstrative Pronouns are used to point out something.   this, that, these, those Demonstratives can also be adjectives. **Examples:** *this* dog, *these* people
Interrogative Pronouns are used to ask a question.   what, which, who, whom, whose
Nominative Pronouns are used as the subject or as a predicate nominative. I, you, he, she, it, we, you, they
Object Pronouns are used in the predicate as a direct object or an object of a preposition. me, you, him, her, it, us, them, whom
Possessive Pronouns show ownership. Some possessive pronouns are used with nouns: my, your, his, her, its, our, your, their, and whose. Other possessive pronouns can stand alone: hers, his, mine, ours, theirs, yours, and whose.
Relative Pronouns are used to relate a clause to an antecedent: that, which, who, whom, and whose.
Indefinite Pronouns replace nouns that are not specific.
Singular: another, each, everything, nobody, other, anybody, either, little, no one, somebody, anyone, everybody, much, nothing, someone, anything, everyone, neither, one, something
Plural: both, few, many, others, and several
Singular and Plural: all, any, more, most, none, and some.
Reflexive Pronouns and **Intensive Pronouns** are the same: myself, yourself, himself, herself, itself, ourselves, yourselves, and themselves. The <u>uses</u> of reflexive and intensive pronouns are different.
A **reflexive pronoun** is <u>essential</u>; it cannot be removed without changing the meaning of the sentence. A reflexive pronoun is used to avoid awkwardly repeating the noun or pronoun antecedent within the sentence. **Example:** Maureen treated *herself* to a relaxing walk along the beach.
An **intensive pronoun** emphasizes a noun or another pronoun in a sentence; however, it is <u>non-essential</u>. An intensive pronoun can be removed without changing the meaning of the sentence. **Example:** The firefighters, *themselves*, had installed the smoke detectors.

Verbs:
Action Verbs show action or possession.
Transitive Verbs are action verbs that send action to a direct object. **Example:** Pat *reads* the *newspaper* every morning. (verb → reads; direct object → newspaper)
Intransitive Verbs are action verbs that have no direct object. **Example:** Pat *reads* all the time. (verb → reads; no direct object)
Verbs of Being (Forms of *be*) do not show action; they can act as linking or helping verbs. is, are, was, were, be, am, being, been
Linking Verbs do not show action; they show a condition. **Examples:** appear, become, feel, seem, smell, taste, sounds, and all forms of *be*.
Auxiliary (Helping) Verbs are used with other verbs to form a verb phrase. **Examples:** is, are, was, were, be, am, being, been, might, could, should, would, can, do, does, did, may, must, will, shall, have, has, had
Verb Tense tells the time when the action or condition of the verb occurs. There are fourteen tenses (see the Verb Conjugation chart on page 67). The <u>basic</u> verb tenses are past, present, and future. For a chart of Perfect Tenses of verbs, see p. 66.

Help Pages

Irregular Verbs:		
Present	**Past**	**Past Participle**
bear	bore	*has, have, or had* born
beat	beat	*has, have, or had* beaten
bend	bent	*has, have, or had* bent
bid	bid / bade	*has, have, or had* bid / bidden
bind	bound	*has, have, or had* bound
burst	burst	*has, have, or had* burst
cut	cut	*has, have, or had* cut
dream	dreamed / dreamt	*has, have, or had* dreamed / dreamt
fit	fit	*has, have, or had* fit
fling	flung	*has, have, or had* flung
forsake	forsook	*has, have, or had* forsaken
hit	hit	*has, have, or had* hit
hurt	hurt	*has, have, or had* hurt
knit	knit	*has, have, or had* knit
leap	leaped / leapt	*has, have, or had* leaped / leapt
learn	learned	*has, have, or had* learned
lend	lent	*has, have, or had* lent
lose	lost	*has, have, or had* lost
sew	sewed	*has, have, or had* sewed / sewn
shave	shaved	*has, have, or had* shaved
show	showed	*has, have, or had* showed / shown
sink	sank	*has, have, or had* sunk
sling	slung	*has, have, or had* slung
spring	sprang / sprung	*has, have, or had* sprung
uphold	upheld	*has, have, or had* upheld
weave	weaved / wove	*has, have, or had* weaved / woven
withhold	withheld	*has, have, or had* withheld

Perfect Tenses:

There are three perfect verb tenses in English. They all use past tense verbs plus the helping verbs, *has*, *have*, or *had*.

	Present Perfect	**Past Perfect**	**Future Perfect**
Use of the Verb	Shows action that is ongoing or indefinite.	Shows which thing happened first. (Both happened in the past.)	Shows what will happen before something else in the future.
Helping Verbs	*has* or *have*	*had*	*will have*
Example (Singular Subject)	Lori *has finished* the reports.	Ricky *had played* on another team.	Tristan *will have eaten* lunch by noon.
Example (Plural Subject)	The coaches *have scheduled* the try-outs.	The Fitzgeralds *had traveled* through Europe.	The girls *will have sold* all the magazines by then.

Help Pages

Complete Verb Conjugation:

A complete verb conjugation shows all 14 tenses with the singular and plural nominative pronouns. Below is the complete conjugation chart for the irregular verb *show*.

Verb Form	Singular	Plural
Past	I showed. You showed. He / She / It showed.	We showed. You showed. They showed.
Present	I show. You show. He / She / It shows.	We show. You show. They show.
Future	I will show. You will show. He / She / It will show.	We will show. You will show. They will show.
Past Perfect	I had shown. You had shown. He / She / It had shown.	We had shown. You had shown. They had shown.
Present Perfect	I have shown. You have shown. He / She / It has shown.	We have shown. You have shown. They have shown.
Future Perfect	I will have shown. You will have shown. He / She / It will have shown.	We will have shown. You will have shown. They will have shown.
Past Progressive	I was showing. You were showing. He / She / It was showing.	We were showing. You were showing. They were showing.
Present Progressive	I am showing. You are showing. He / She / It is showing.	We are showing. You are showing. They are showing.
Future Progressive	I will be showing. You will be showing. He / She / It will be showing.	We will be showing. You will be showing. They will be showing.
Past Perfect Progressive	I had been showing. You had been showing. He / She / It had been showing.	We had been showing. You had been showing. They had been showing.
Present Perfect Progressive	I have been showing. You have been showing. He / She / It has been showing.	We have been showing. You have been showing. They have been showing.
Future Perfect Progressive	I will have been showing. You will have been showing. He / She / It will have been showing.	We will have been showing. You will have been showing. They will have been showing.
Emphatic Past	I did show. You did show. He / She / It did show.	We did show. You did show. They did show.
Emphatic Present	I do show. You do show. He / She / It does show.	We do show. You do show. They do show.

Help Pages

Sentences:

Sentence Types: Declarative, Exclamatory, Interrogative, and Imperative.

Structure	Parts	Joined by	Example
Simple	subject & predicate	---	Winter is a great time to try downhill skiing.
Compound	two or more independent clauses	coordinate conjunction (and, but, or)	You can use your own skis, *or* you can rent all your gear at a ski resort.
Complex	subordinate and main clause	subordinating conjunction	You may want to do some sledding *if* downhill skiing is too scary.
Compound - Complex	two or more main clauses and one or more subordinate clauses	conjunctions (both coordinate & subordinating)	Snowboarding is also lots of fun, *and* it's pretty easy *as long as* you have good balance.

Editing Marks:

Capital letter	≡	Take something out	ℐ
End punctuation	⊙ ! ?	Check spelling	sp
Add something	∧	Indent	¶
Change to lower case	/		

Prefixes, Suffixes, and Roots (Oh my!):

	Meaning		Meaning		Meaning		Meaning
acous, audio	hearing, listening	*circum*	around	*ig, igni*	burning	*pan*	all
		contra	against	*macr, macro*	large	*pass*	feeling
a, an	not, without	*crypt, crypto*	secret	*magni, mag*	large	*path*	strong emotion
amphi	both	*dem, demo*	people	*major*	large	*ped, pedi*	foot
ampli	large	*dict*	speak	*maxi*	large	*photo*	light
anthropo	human	*dis*	not	*meg, megalo*	large	*poly*	many
anti	against	*ethno*	people	*megal, mega*	large	*popu*	people
aqua	water	*frag, frac*	break	*meta*	between	*pyro*	fire
bi	two	*flam*	fire	*meter*	measure	*recti*	straight, right
biblio	book	*geo*	earth	*mono*	one	*rupt*	break
bio	life	*grand*	large	*morph*	form	*scrib*	write
caca	bad	*graph, gram*	written	*omni*	all	*syn*	same
caus	fire	*hemi*	half	*neo*	new	*tempo*	time
chromo	color	*hydra, hydro*	water	*ology*	study of	*tempor*	time
chrono	time	*hydr, hyd*	water	*onym*	name	*theo*	religion, god

Help Pages

Punctuation Rules:

Commas

1. Use commas to separate words, phrases, or clauses in a series.
   Examples: Words → leaves, twigs, seeds, and grass
   Phrases → running errands, buying groceries, or cleaning the garage
   Clauses → Jill wrote the draft, Harry edited it, and Marcie read the final copy.

2. Use commas to separate adjectives that describe *in the same way* – do not use commas to separate adjectives that describe in different ways.
   Example: a *cold, snowy* day   *two large* reindeer

3. Use commas to separate consecutive words and numbers, for example, when writing dates and names of cities (addresses). Use a comma <u>before</u> and <u>after</u> a professional title that follows a name within a sentence.
   Examples: Freemont, Alabama   Thursday, February 15, 2007   Dr. Lois Walker, M.D.,

4. Use a comma to separate two independent clauses joined by a *coordinate conjunction* (as in a compound sentence).
   Example: I brought a lunch, but Janie forgot hers. I shared my sandwich, and Georgie gave her some chips.

5. Use commas to set off anything that "interrupts" a sentence. An example is given for each.
   Appositives → This hat, my father's favorite, has been around since before I was born.
   Adjectives that follow nouns → The hat, tattered and worn, hangs on a hook above the coats.
   Contrasting phrases → Dad always wore a hat, not earmuffs, when the weather was cold.
   Conjunctive adverbs → (also, besides, furthermore, however, indeed, instead, moreover, nevertheless, otherwise, therefore, thus); Furthermore, he wore a hat in almost any kind of weather. It suited him, however.
   Any non-essential component, such as a non-restrictive modifier;
   My father's hat, which is made of wool, was imported from Ireland.

6. Use a comma after an introductory word (direct address, interjection, etc.), clause, or phrase (especially if the phrase contains more than four words).
   Examples: Interjection → Look, it's starting to rain. Incidentally, here is the umbrella you left at my house.
   Direct Address → Phillip, close the door.
   Clause → Since it is raining, we may not be able to go.
   Phrase → On the other hand, we could take the bus.

7. Use a comma before quotation marks if there is no other punctuation mark.
   Example: Fred replied, "I never do the same thing twice."

8. Use a comma after the salutation in a personal letter and after the closing in any letter.
   Examples: Dear Renee,   Sincerely yours,   Yours truly,

Quotation Marks

1. Always put someone's words inside quotation marks. All the punctuation that goes with the statement goes inside the quotation marks.
   Example: Gina said, "Meet me at three."

2. When writing a dialogue, put the speaker's words in quotation marks, and begin a new paragraph with each new speaker.
   Example: "Hello, Dennis," beamed Lucy.
   "What are you doing here?" exclaimed Dennis.
   "Don't worry – I'm not following you," laughed Lucy.

3. Use quotation marks to indicate the title of a short story, book chapter, song, poem, or article.
   Examples: We read "The Tortoise and the Hare," one of Aesop's famous fables. Eliza is singing "Twinkle, Twinkle Little Star."

Help Pages

Quotation Marks (continued)
4. Use quotation marks to indicate slang words.   **Example:** I'm exhausted; I've been working "24/7."
5. To set apart words which are already in quotes, use single quotation marks.   **Examples:** "Let's read 'Three Blind Mice,' " she said. Mary asked, "Did she say 'hello' or not?"
Apostrophes

1. Use an apostrophe with the letter –s to show possession.
   Examples: **Singular Possessive** → the farm's equipment, the man's home
   Plural Possessive → the apples' stems, the vegetables' colors
   Compound Possessive → Larry and Ed's company   (They both own the company.)
   More than one owner → Sue's and Ivory's projects   (They each have a project.)

2. Use an apostrophe to show that letters have been left out, as in contractions.
   Examples: **Contractions** → can't, aren't, he's, shouldn't, I'll, they're
   Other words → four o'clock, the blizzard of '07, 'twas the night before, o'er the hill

3. Use an apostrophe to make an individual letter, number, or symbol plural.
   Examples: Today we learned how to write our *2's* and *t's*. Morgan eats *BLT's* for lunch.
   What do those *#'s* mean? Use *%'s* when you write your answers.

Semicolons
1. Use a semicolon to connect two independent clauses. The semicolon replaces a coordinate conjunction, so do not use both.
2. Use a semicolon instead of a comma to separate items that already have commas.   **Example:** Monday, March 5; Tuesday, April 10; and Wednesday, April 16
Colons
1. Use a colon – after an independent clause – to introduce a list. Do not use the colon after a verb or preposition.   **Example:** The ingredients are fairly simple: tomatoes, garlic, basil, and oregano.
2. Use a colon to introduce a lengthy quotation, or to introduce a quotation that is not preceded by a form of *said*. Place the colon before the quotation marks.   **Example:** Lincoln began his speech: "Four score and seven years ago our fathers brought forth on this continent, a new nation, conceived in Liberty, and dedicated to the proposition that all men are created equal."

3. Use a colon to separate independent clauses if you want to add emphasis.
   Example: Paula tried something new: Instead of borrowing the book, she downloaded it.
   *Notice that the clause after the colon begins with a capital letter.

4. Use a colon after the salutation in a business letter.   **Examples:** To Whom this May Concern: Dear Madam:
Dashes, Parentheses, Brackets, and Ellipses

1. A dash is twice the length of a hyphen. Use dashes to add words (like appositives) within a sentence or at the end of a sentence. A dash is used for emphasis and should not be used very often.
   Examples: **Within a Sentence** → The final competition – a stressful affair – begins immediately.
   At the End of a Sentence → Tomorrow is a big day – the finalists will be announced.

2. Use dashes instead of commas when too many commas make a sentence unclear.
   Examples: **Unclear** → There are several companies, Atlas Movers in Chicago, Illinois, for example, that do a great job.
   Clear → There are several companies – Atlas Movers in Chicago, Illinois, for example – that do a great job.

Help Pages

Dashes, Parentheses, Brackets and Ellipses (continued)
3. Use parentheses to add information that is relevant but not essential to the sentence. Parentheses can be used in the same way as dashes, but they are less emphatic. Notice that the end punctuation goes outside of the parentheses. **Examples:** Uncle Larry (my dad's brother) is a zoologist. He also lives in the city (New York).
4. When a complete sentence is inside parentheses, it should begin with a capital and end with an end mark. Otherwise, do not capitalize or punctuate within parentheses. **Examples:** We visited the Bahamas in 1998. (That was our first trip together.)
5. Use parentheses to set apart numbers or lettered choices. **Examples:** 1) Rudy 2) Clara 3) Tim   Choose one: a) library b) post office c) city hall
6. An ellipsis lets the reader know that something (words or numbers) is missing. An ellipsis may come at the beginning, middle, or end of a sentence; it is often used in quotations. **Examples: Quotation** → "Now we are engaged in a great civil war…It is altogether fitting and proper that we should do this…" ~Abraham Lincoln, 1863 **Number Set** → See numbers 23, 24, 25,…,100.
7. Brackets have limited usage. Use brackets to insert something that is already in parentheses. **Example:** (The Gettysburg Address [November 19, 1863] was delivered in Gettysburg, Pennsylvania.)
8. Use brackets around the word *sic,* a Latin word that shows a mistake is acknowledged by the writer. **Example:** Her answer was, "You ain't seen nothin' [sic] yet!"
Hyphens
1. Use a hyphen between the tens and the ones place, when writing out the numbers twenty-one through ninety-nine. **Examples:** forty-two   seventy-six
2. Use a hyphen when writing fractions. **Example:** three-fifths   two-thirds
3. Use a hyphen to separate words on two lines. The word must be separated by syllables, and each syllable should have at least two letters. (Whenever possible, avoid separation of words in this way.)
4. Use a hyphen to join a prefix with a base word. The hyphen helps make the word more clear. **Examples:** co-captains   ex-mayor   non-taxable
5. Use a hyphen in some compound words. **Examples:** well-rounded   president-elect

Capitalization Rules:
1. Capitalize the first word in any sentence – including sentences within quotation marks and complete sentences which follow a colon. Capitalize interjections.
2. Capitalize all proper nouns. This includes the names of people, pets, and buildings.
3. Capitalize the names of places: geographical locations, oceans, rivers, lakes, streets, cities, states, regions, countries, and continents.
4. Capitalize all proper adjectives.
5. Capitalize social titles.
6. Capitalize the names of historic events and time periods, monuments, and documents. **Examples:** Gettysburg Address   Roaring Twenties   Sears Tower   Articles of Confederation

Help Pages

Capitalization Rules (continued):
7. Capitalize the days of the week, months, and holidays.
8. Always capitalize the pronoun, *I*.
9. Capitalize the first word and every important word in a title.
10. Some abbreviations are capitalized; others are not.
11. Capitalize the first word in the greeting and the first word in the closing of a letter.

Spelling Rules:
Rules for Forming Plurals
1. Words ending in *s*, *x*, *z*, *ch*, or *sh*, add *–es* to make the plural.
2. Many words that end in *–f* or *–fe* form the plural by changing the *–f* or *–fe* to *–ves*. (thief → thieves) Some nouns that end in *–f* or *–ff* do not follow the rule for making plurals. (cliff → cliffs, belief → beliefs)
3. Some nouns that end in a consonant + *-o* form the plural by adding *–s* (tattoo → tattoos); others add *–es*. (veto → vetoes)
4. Some nouns do not add *–s* or *–es* to form the plural; these irregular plurals must be memorized. (phenomenon → phenomena)
5. Some nouns have the same form whether they are singular or plural. (deer, grapefruit, salmon)
6. Some nouns have only a plural form, and they always take a plural verb. (scissors, pants, dues)
7. Some nouns are singular even though they end in *–s*; they take singular verbs. (mumps, economics, atlas)
Other Spelling Rules
8. Place *i* before *e*, except after *c*, or when sounded like *ā* as in *neighbor* and *weigh*. (mischief, eight)
9. Regular verbs show past tense by adding *–ed*. (stop → stopped) Irregular verbs change their spelling in the past tense. See the Irregular Verbs chart on p. 66.
10. When adding a prefix to a word, do not change the spelling of the prefix or the root. (mis- + step → misstep)
11. If a word ends in a vowel and *–y*, add a suffix without changing the spelling of the word. (employ + -er → employer)
12. If a word ends in a consonant + *-y*, change the *y* to *i* before adding suffixes such as *-es*, *-er*, *-ed*, or *-est*. (try → tried) If the suffix begins with an *-i*, do not change the *-y* to *-i*. (hurry → hurrying)

Person:
Writing will be in the first, second, or third person.
First Person refers to the speaker or writer. Use the pronouns *I*, *me*, *my*, *mine*, *myself*, *we*, *us*, *our*, *ours*, and *ourselves* when writing or speaking in first person.   **Example:** I brought my dog to the animal hospital.
Second Person refers to the reader or listener, the one being spoken to. Use the pronouns *you*, *your*, *yours*, and *yourself* when speaking or writing in the second person.   **Example:** You have an appointment with your tutor.

Help Pages

Person (continued):
Third Person is the thing or person being described or spoken about. For third person, use the pronouns *he, she, it, him, her, himself, herself, itself, his, her, hers, its, their, theirs, they, them*, and *themselves*. Third person is the most appropriate point of view for term papers, reports, articles, and essays. **Example:** The mothers watched their children playing.
Notice that the idea of "person" is very important for subject-verb agreement and pronoun agreement. The "person" should not change within the same piece of writing.

Verbals:
Participles, gerunds, and infinitives are called verbals because they are formed from verbs. A summary of verbals can be found in Lesson #9.
Participles are verbs that act as adjectives. Participles modify nouns or pronouns. In the example below, *barking* modifies *dog* and *experienced* modifies *patrol officer*. **Example:** A <u>barking</u> dog alerted the <u>experienced</u> patrol officer.   present participle   past participle

A **gerund** is a verb ending in -ing that is used as a noun.
Since a gerund acts as a noun, it may be a subject, predicate nominative, direct object, indirect object, or object of a preposition.
Examples: Subject → <u>Knitting</u> is my grandmother's favorite pastime.
                Predicate Nominative → My pleasure is <u>cooking</u>.
                Direct Object → Dad enjoys <u>golfing</u>.
                Indirect Object → Someday, I will give <u>painting</u> a try.
                Object of a Preposition → I have had some success with <u>drawing</u>.

An **infinitive** is the word *to* plus the simple present tense form of a verb. An infinitive may function as a noun, an adjective, or an adverb.

Part of Speech	Function	Examples
noun	subject	<u>To succeed</u> takes patience.
noun	predicate noun	Grandpa's desire is <u>to dance</u>.
noun	direct object	Millie likes <u>to garden</u>.
noun	object of a preposition	I could think of nothing to do except <u>to scream</u>.
adjective	modifies a noun / pronoun	In the library there is so *much* <u>to read</u>!
adverb	modifies a verb	<u>To apply</u>, *complete* this form.
adverb	modifies an adjective	Phyllis was *happy* <u>to see</u> you.
adverb	modifies an adverb	It was too late *even* <u>to try</u>.

Help Pages

How to Fix a Run-on Sentence:

A **run-on sentence** has two or more independent clauses which are not properly joined.
Example: Today we had planned to go on a picnic it rained all afternoon!

- **Separate two independent clauses into two sentences.**   Today we had planned to go on a picnic. It rained all afternoon!
- **Insert a semicolon between the two independent clauses.**   Today we had planned to go on a picnic; it rained all afternoon!
- **Insert a semicolon between the two independent clauses and add a transitional word (therefore, moreover, for example, etc.) and a comma.**   Today we had planned to go on a picnic; however, it rained all afternoon!
- **Insert a comma and a coordinating conjunction between the two independent clauses.**   Today we had planned to go on a picnic, but it rained all afternoon!
- **Rewrite the sentence using a subordinating conjunction to separate the two independent clauses.**   Although we had planned to go on a picnic today, it rained all afternoon!

Avoiding Plagiarism:

What is plagiarism? **Plagiarism is the illegal use of someone else's written or spoken words.** Plagiarism can take many forms:

- copying another student's work (even with permission) to hand in for credit;
- allowing someone else to write your paper;
- downloading a paper from the Internet and handing it in for credit;
- using someone else's words or ideas without giving proper credit; and/or
- failing to properly cite sources in a written bibliography.

As you prepare for high school and beyond, you will be required to write papers based on research. You will want to include information from outside **sources:** books, encyclopedias, periodicals, interviews, film documentaries, and the Worldwide Web. Any information – words, ideas, graphics, etc. – that comes from anyone other than you must be *cited* within the text and in a bibliography. **A bibliography is a list of sources that were used to get information for your paper.**

When doing research for an assignment, be sure to write down authors' names, titles of publications, dates, and whatever other information is required by your teacher. These details will help you to write the **citations** for your bibliography. **A citation is a list of the details needed to find the full source of information used in your paper.** A citation always includes the author's name if it is available. If your teacher does not have a specific guide for you to follow, you can use the Bibliography guide on the next page of this book.

Quoting Someone

If you want to use someone's exact words in your writing, always include the speaker's name, and put the words in quotation marks. If you want to use information that you saw on TV, read in a book, or found online, make sure you put the information in your own words, and cite the source in your bibliography. Remember, you can use information from any source as long as the information is properly cited.

Help Pages

Bibliography:
A bibliography lists sources in alphabetical order. The author's name, title of the book, magazine, or internet article is included, as well as the publisher, date of publication, and sometimes page numbers. Most teachers prefer to have students set up a bibliography in a certain way. You should follow your teacher's directions for setting up a bibliography. Here are some examples of how to list various sources.

Book:
    Author's last name, first name. <u>Title of Book</u>. City: Publisher, Date.
Example:
    Lawry, Matthew. <u>Fascinating Desert Life Forms</u>. Dayton: Traders Press, 2004.

Encyclopedia: <u>Title of Encyclopedia</u>, Date. Volume Number, "Title of Article," page numbers. **Example:**   <u>Universe Encyclopedia</u>, 2006. Vol. 3, "Deserts," pp. 19-23.

Magazine Article:
    Author's last name, first name, "Article Title." <u>Name of Magazine</u>. Volume Number, (Date): page numbers.
Example:
    Phillips, Carla, "My Days in the Sahara." <u>Geography and More</u>. Vol. 18, No. 3, (Fall 2000): pp. 3-5.

Internet Article:
    Author's name, (Date). Title. <u>Electronic Forum</u> (Online). Email address, if available.
Example:
    Tasha Green, (March 9, 2004). Desert Life. <u>Topics to Research</u> (Online). homeworkhelp@singleton.com.

World Wide Web: URL. Author or name of item, date. **Example:**   <u>http://www.learnaboutdeserts.com</u>. Lisa King, June 1, 2006.

Personal Interview:
    Person's last name, first name. Occupation. Date of interview.
Example:
    Journeyman, James. Zoologist. February 20, 2007.

Level 8

English Grammar
& Writing Mechanics

Answers to Lessons

Lesson #1		Lesson #2		Lesson #3	
1	verb	1	Imperative	1	Bright red, white, and blue decorations
2	noun	2	Exclamatory	2	B
3	preposition	3	Interrogative	3	D
4	pronoun	4	Declarative	4	✓ A) ✓ C)
5	adverb	5	Six out of every ten kids / drink…	5	asked saw (be) (was)
6	adjective	6	(were) ready	6	outside beyond throughout over
7	conjunction	7	she and I	7	(willow) with its long flowing branches
8	interjection	8	him	8 - 12	Answers will vary.
9	D	9	(curious) (inquisitive)		
10	comparatives – 2 superlatives – 3 or more	10	should arrive helping main		
11	A				
12	capitalize ≡ add something ∧ take something out ꝺ add end mark ⊙ ! ? indent ¶ make lower case /	11 - 12	A) clause C) phrase B) phrase D) clause		

Lesson #4		Lesson #5		Lesson #6	
1	(houses) along the lake	1	B	1	S - telephone P - websites
2	B	2	plagiarism	2	S - George P - Hawaiians
3	red, green, yellow beautiful	3	bibliography	3	S - officer's P - women's
4	D. obj. of a preposition C. pred. adjective A. subject B. linking verb	4	periodical, internet, personal interview (Answers may vary.)	4	S - Melissa's P - Virginians'
5	subject verb (predicate)	5	at the new Welcome Center	5	They had seen. They have seen. They will have seen.
6	sits atop a forested hill	6	A) at C) map B) Welcome Center	6	A
7	~~I~~ me	7	He you their they	7	(handed) me envelope
8	~~there~~ their	8	the captain's quarters the children's playground	8	~~are~~ is
9	~~seen~~ saw or have seen	9	street, large, away,	9	(girls) who ran the carwash
10	photo photography telephoto	10	we, you, they	10 - 12	A) team B) freshly C) entire D) brings E) their F) or
11	ped pedestrian biped	11	me, you, him, her, it		
12	hemi hemisphere hemiplegia	12	show ownership		

	Lesson #7		Lesson #8		Lesson #9
1	C	1	Felix, the restaurant owner, has…	1	(bird) its
2	is practicing	2	…coasters, not the merry-go-rounds!	2	at the office counter modifies sheet
3	opinion	3	Look,…Let's get in line, so…	3	participle
4	A	4	was chased (police)	4	verb
5	planted	5	(flew) out of the park	5	gerund
6	A The tigers… P All of the…	6	where	6	S Guess what! S School is cancelled. F And all activities!
7	independent	7	A) dict C) fract B) chromo D) contra	7	D
8	(All) of the apples near the top of the tree			8	is is
9	mr. frost yes i'll	8 - 12	Answers will vary.	9	A. auxiliary B. action C. action D. linking E. auxiliary
10 - 12	A) signed B) abbreviating C) select D) selected E) shoveled F) shoveling			10	D
				11	A
				12	C

Summer Solutions© Grammar & Writing — Level 8

	Lesson #10		Lesson #11		Lesson #12
1	they (musicians)	1	her	1	Spending a few days at Disney World — A
2	A	2	has	2	A (few) ~~of the girls on my softball team~~
3	two	3	his	3	will have been televised
4	I	4	P The muffins… A and people…	4	(view) from the front of the house
5	T	5	metaphor	5	…city; the park…
6	gingerly magnificent carefully exotic	6	adjectives nouns or pronouns	6	personification
7	adjectives – magnificent, exotic adverbs – gingerly, carefully	7	participle	7	A) P B) V C) P
8	It rotated. It rotates. It will rotate. It had rotated.	8	gerund	8	B
9	It has rotated. It will have rotated. It was rotating.	9	verb	9	verb, adjective, adverb
10	It is rotating. It will be rotating. It had been rotating.	10	three or more	10–12	B. appositive A. simple subject D. predicate nominative C. linking verb F. direct object E. transitive verb
11	It has been rotating. It will have been rotating.	11	african (capitalize A)		
12	It did rotate. It does rotate.	12	A) syn B) hydro C) onym		

	Lesson #13		Lesson #14		Lesson #15
1	"Would you like to try the Alaskan whitefish?" asked the waiter.	1	A	1	pleasing the new boss — object of a preposition
2	...everything: party favors, hats, games, and food!	2	gardening painting — direct objects	2	The boys' 100% cotton shirts are on sale today.
3	(although) subordinating	3	A) half C) time B) book	3	idiom
4	Shopping	4	compound-complex	4	C
5	subject	5	(watch) until I get home	5-7	F. obj. of a preposition C. participle E. preposition B. direct object A. progressive verb D. infinitive
6	Daily exercise keeps the animals in the Nature Exhibit mentally and physically engaged.	6	As soon as you finish eating (wash)		
7	Several of the varieties of food served on the cruise (S)	7	to drink modifies "something"		
8	To operate adverb	8-12	Answers will vary.	8	She watched. She watches. She will watch.
9	to wear adjective			9	She had watched. She has watched. She will have watched.
10	to remember noun			10	She was watching. She is watching. She will be watching.
11	A. secret B. right C. deity			11	She had been watching. She has been watching. She will have been watching.
12	(Dad) himself			12	She did watch. She does watch.

	Lesson #16		Lesson #17		Lesson #18
1	A. caca C. morph B. anthropo	1	B	1	noun
2	…to Dr. Sally Green, Ph.D., at… Cloverleaf,…	2	B	2	In the new kitchen, Felicia can watch the birds while she is washing dishes.
3	<u>apprehensively</u> modifies approached	3	The committee elected its new chairman today.	3	gave (runners) [water and snacks]
4	<u>Driving</u> subject	4	C	4	will have traveled
5	(Most) ~~of the pictures in our yearbook~~	5	…problems; there…	5	adverb
6	and, or, nor, but, so, for, yet	6	A	6	Example: Every year we go to a theme park, and although we always have a great time, I really want to visit the Grand Canyon.
7	personification	7	<u>because</u> subordinating	7	<u>when she applies herself</u> modifies excels
8	(Their)[sp] <u>molly</u> /been have	8	A	8	(fence) <u>that separates our properties</u>
9	C if we win P next to the goal line	9	verb - stands simple subject - tree	9	3 clauses compound-complex
10-12	A) 6. B) 5. C) 2. D) 4. E) 3. F) 1.	10	<u>To transfer calls</u> adverb	10	[may reach] [will need] [are]
		11	<u>to remove the tire</u> noun	11	whose
		12	<u>to serve with dinner</u> adjective	12	Summer = western hemisphere =

83

	Lesson #19		Lesson #20		Lesson #21
1	A. fire B. measure C. writing	1	needs	1	Wilde, Oscar. <u>The Happy Prince and Other Fairy Tales</u>. New York: Courier Dover Publications, 2001.
2	than they	2	Answers will vary.	2	inner being
3	C	3	B	3	simile
4	both	4	<u>litter</u>	4	gerund
5	opinion	5	deer	5	participle
6	fact	6	you ~~yourself~~	6	verb
7	<u>to learn</u> adjective	7	Danish ~~danish~~	7	<u>To build a new house</u> B
8-12	Answers will vary.	8	They studied. They study. They will study. They had studied.	8	did find
		9	They have studied. They will have studied. They were studying.	9	elder, youngest
				10	C
		10	They are studying. They will be studying. They had been studying.	11	Arlington National Cemetery is a burial ground for American soldiers.
		11	They have been studying. They will have been studying.	12	The Arlington estate in Virginia once belonged to General Robert E. Lee.
		12	They did study. They do study.		

Summer Solutions Grammar & Writing — Level 8

	Lesson #22		Lesson #23		Lesson #24
1	~~their~~ its	1	D	1	new D) one A) fire C) hearing B)
2	(girl) running the ice cream stand	2	complex	2	to order new carpet direct object
3	Answers will vary.	3	(so) coordinate	3	to schedule events predicate nominative
4	Answers will vary.	4	D	4	compound-complex
5	Answers will vary.	5	book title, author's name, publisher, city, date	5	A
6	I	6	A	6	A
7	you ~~yourself~~	7	Just then, a delivery man with a double-cheese pizza rang the doorbell.	7	Dancing subject
8	Canadian ~~canadian~~	8	woke (children)		
9	P We were… A and…	9	noun		
10	(coarse) sp (comunity) sp course community	10	too ~~to~~		
11-12	Hearing: audiologist Feet: pedicure, moped Secrets: cryptology, cryptic Time: temporal, chronological Fire: pyrotechnics, ignition, flambeau	11	me ~~myself~~	8-12	Answers will vary.
		12	(was) president		

	Lesson #25		Lesson #26		Lesson #27
1	C	1	(became) president	1	gone (went)
2	(One) of the goals of the event	2	B	2	he (him)
3	noun	3	A herd of buffalo grazing on the open plain/was...	3	clearly (clear)
4	typing letters answering calls packing boxes predicate nominatives	4	trophies wolves slices	4	independent
5	At North Park, we rode all the roller coasters at least three times.	5	she	5	verb
6	B	6	A	6	french while (desert)ˢᵖ
7	A police officer on horse back chased a stray dog through the neighborhood.	7	german Birthday	7	A
8 - 12	He trusted. He trusts. He will trust. He had trusted. He has trusted. He will have trusted. He was trusting. He is trusting. He will be trusting. He had been trusting. He has been trusting. He will have been trusting. He did trust. He does trust.	8	(vanilla)ˢᵖ coffee.	8	burst burst burst
		9	Sanchez, artist, singer, leader, 30, Laredo,	9	forsake forsook forsaking
		10 - 12	proper adjective C. infinitive phrase F. prepositional phrase E. conjunction D. appositive A. passive verb B.	10	spring springing sprung
				11 - 12	Answers will vary.

Summer Solutions© Grammar & Writing — Level 8

	Lesson #28		Lesson #29		Lesson #30
1-4	H. infinitive F. transitive verb A. subject G. direct object B. predicate nominative E. gerund phrase D. prepositional phrase C. passive verb	1	3 clauses compound-complex	1	metaphor
		2	<u>verb</u>: <u>direct object</u> pack trunk embrace friends	2	C
		3	embark, wake, fled	3	A first grader with a piece of birthday cake came to the door while Mrs. Sherman was writing on the board.
		4	is	4	(bought) us [stick]
5	compound	5	fact	5	D
6	simple	6	both	6	chrono, tempo
7	complex	7	opinion	7	grand, magni
8	<u>bathes</u> (countryside)	8-12	Answers will vary.	8	acous, audio
9	D			9	syn, homo
10	You			10	anti, contra
11	A. gerund phrase B. verb and direct object			11-12	A. gerund subject B. infinitive adverb C. infinitive adverb D. gerund subject
12	preposition				